catalog
of
unabashed
gratitude

pitt poetry series

•

Ed Ochester, Editor

catalog
of
unabashed
gratitude

•

ross gay

university of pittsburgh press

Published by the University of Pittsburgh Press, Pittsburgh, Pa., 15260

Manufactured in the United States of America

Printed on acid-free paper

20 19 18 17 16

ISBN 13: 978-0-8229-6331-8

ISBN 10: 0-8229-6331-0

for Stephanie Smith and Judy Gay

contents

catalog
of
unabashed
gratitude

to the fig tree on 9th and christian

Tumbling through the
city in my
mind without once
looking up
the racket in
the lugwork probably
rehearsing some
stupid thing I
said or did
some crime or
other the city they
say is a lonely
place until yes
the sound of sweeping
and a woman
yes with a
broom beneath
which you are now
too the canopy
of a fig its
arms pulling the
September sun to it
and she
has a hose too
and so works hard

rinsing and scrubbing
the walk
lest some poor sod
slip on the
silk of a fig
and break his hip
and not probably
reach over to gobble up
the perpetrator
the light catches
the veins in her hands
when I ask about
the tree they
flutter in the air and
she says take
as much as
you can
help me
so I load my
pockets and mouth
and she points
to the step-ladder against
the wall to
mean more but
I was without a

sack so my meager
plunder would have to
suffice and an old woman
whom gravity
was pulling into
the earth loosed one
from a low slung
branch and its eye
wept like hers
which she dabbed
with a kerchief as she
cleaved the fig with
what remained of her
teeth and soon there were
eight or nine
people gathered beneath
the tree looking into
it like a
constellation pointing
do you see it
and I am tall and so
good for these things
and a bald man even
told me so
when I grabbed three

or four for
him reaching into the
giddy throngs of
yellow-jackets sugar
stoned which he only
pointed to smiling and
rubbing his stomach
I mean he was really rubbing his stomach
like there was a baby
in there
it was hot his
head shone while he
offered recipes to the
group using words which
I couldn't understand and besides
I was a little
tipsy on the dance
of the velvety heart rolling
in my mouth
pulling me down and
down into the
oldest countries of my
body where I ate my first fig
from the hand of a man who escaped his country
by swimming through the night

and maybe
never said more than
five words to me
at once but gave me
figs and a man on his way
to work hops twice
to reach at last his
fig which he smiles at and calls
baby, *c'mere baby*,
he says and blows a kiss
to the tree which everyone knows
cannot grow this far north
being Mediterranean
and favoring the rocky, sunbaked soils
of Jordan and Sicily
but no one told the fig tree
or the immigrants
there is a way
the fig tree grows
in groves it wants,
it seems, to hold us,
yes I am anthropomorphizing
goddammit I have twice
in the last thirty seconds
rubbed my sweaty

forearm into someone else's
sweaty shoulder
gleeful eating out of each other's hands
on Christian St.
in Philadelphia a city like most
which has murdered its own
people
this is true
we are feeding each other
from a tree
at the corner of Christian and 9th
strangers maybe
never again.

ode to buttoning and unbuttoning my shirt

No one knew or at least
I didn't know
they knew
what the thin disks
threaded here
on my shirt
might give me
in terms of joy
this is not something to be taken lightly
the gift
of buttoning one's shirt
slowly
top to bottom
or bottom
to top or sometimes
the buttons
will be on the other
side and
I am a woman
that morning
slipping the glass
through its slot
I tread
differently that day
or some of it

anyway
my conversations
are different
and the car bomb slicing the air
and the people in it
for a quarter mile
and the honeybee's
legs furred with pollen
mean another
thing to me
than on the other days
which too have
been drizzled in this
simplest of joys
in this world
of spaceships and subatomic
this and that
two maybe three
times a day
some days
I have the distinct pleasure
of slowly untethering
the one side
from the other
which is like unbuckling

a stack of vertebrae
with delicacy
for I must only use
the tips
of my fingers
with which I will
one day close
my mother's eyes
this is as delicate
as we can be
in this life
practicing
like this
giving the raft of our hands
to the clumsy spider
and blowing soft until she
lifts her damp heft and
crawls off
we practice like this
pushing the seed into the earth
like this first
in the morning
then at night
we practice
sliding the bones home.

ode to the flute

A man sings
by opening his
mouth a man
sings by opening
his lungs by
turning himself into air
a flute can
be made of a man
nothing is explained
a flute lays
on its side
and prays a wind
might enter it
and make of it
at least
a small final song

burial

You're right, you're right,
the fertilizer's good—
it wasn't a gang of dullards
came up with chucking
a fish in the planting hole
or some midwife got lucky
with the placenta—
oh, I'll plant a tree here!—
and a sudden flush of quince
and jam enough for months—yes,
the magic dust our bodies become
casts spells on the roots
about which someone else
could tell you the chemical processes,
but it's just magic to me,
which is why a couple springs ago
when first putting in my two bare root plum trees
out back I took the jar which has become
my father's house,
and lonely for him and hoping to coax him back
for my mother as much as me,
poured some of him in the planting holes
and he dove in glad for the robust air,
saddling a slight gust
into my nose and mouth,

chuckling as I coughed,
but mostly he disappeared
into the minor yawns in the earth
into which I placed the trees,
splaying wide their roots,
casting the gray dust of my old man
evenly throughout the hole,
replacing then the clods
of dense Indiana soil until the roots
and my father were buried,
watering it in all with one hand
while holding the tree
with the other straight as the flag
to the nation of simple joy
of which my father is now a naturalized citizen,
waving the flag
from his subterranean lair,
the roots curled around him
like shawls or jungle gyms, like
hookahs or the arms of ancestors,
before breast-stroking into the xylem,
riding the elevator up
through the cambium and into the leaves where,
when you put your ear close enough,
you can hear him whisper

good morning, where, if you close your eyes
and push your face you can feel
his stubbly jowls and good lord
this year he was giddy at the first
real fruit set and nestled into the 30 or 40 plums
in the two trees, peering out from the sweet meat
with his hands pressed against the purple skin
like cathedral glass,
and imagine his joy as the sun
wizarded forth those abundant sugars
and I plodded barefoot
and prayerful at the first ripe plum's swell and blush,
almost weepy conjuring
some surely ponderous verse
to convey this bottomless grace,
you know, *oh father oh father* kind of stuff,
hundreds of hot air balloons
filling the sky in my chest, replacing his intubated body
listing like a boat keel side up, replacing
the steady stream of water from the one eye
which his brother wiped before removing the tube,
keeping his hand on the forehead
until the last wind in his body wandered off,
while my brother wailed like an animal,
and my mother said, weeping,

it's ok, it's ok, you can go honey,
at all of which my father
guffawed by kicking from the first bite
buckets of juice down my chin,
staining one of my two button-down shirts,
the salmon-colored silk one, hollering
there's more of that!
almost dancing now in the plum,
in the tree, the way he did as a person,
bent over and biting his lip
and chucking the one hip out
then the other with his elbows cocked
and fists loosely made
and eyes closed and mouth made trumpet
when he knew he could make you happy
just by being a little silly
and sweet.

patience

Call it sloth; call it sleaze;
call it bummery if you please;
I'll call it patience;
I'll call it joy, this,
my supine congress
with the newly yawning grass
and beetles chittering
in their offices
beneath me, as I
nearly drifting to dream
admire this so-called weed which,
if I guarded with teeth bared
my garden of all alien breeds,
if I was all knife and axe
and made a life of hacking
would not have burst gorgeous forth and beckoning
these sort of phallic spires
ringleted by these sort of vaginal blooms
which the new bees, being bees, heed;
and yes, it is spring, if you can't tell
from the words my mind makes
of the world, and everything
makes me mildly or more
hungry—the worm turning
in the leaf mold; the pear blooms

howling forth their pungence
like a choir of wet-dreamed boys
hiking up their skirts; even
the neighbor cat's shimmy
through the grin in the fence,
and the way this bee
before me after whispering
in my ear dips her head
into those dainty lips
not exactly like one entering a chapel
and friends
as if that wasn't enough
blooms forth with her forehead dusted pink
like she has been licked
and so blessed
by the kind of God
to whom this poem is prayer.

ode to the puritan in me

There is a puritan in me
the brim of whose
hat is so sharp
it could cut
your tongue out
with a brow
so furrowed you
could plant beets
or turnips or
something of course
good for storing
he has not taken a nap
since he was two years old
because he detests
sloth above all
he is maybe the only real person
I've ever heard
say "sloth" or "detest"
in conversation
he reads poetry
the puritan in me
with an X-Acto knife in his calloused hand
if not a stick of dynamite
and if the puritan in me sees
two cats making

whoopee in the barn
I think not
because they get
in the way
or scare the cows
but more precisely
because he thinks it is worthless
the angles of animals
fucking freely
in the open air
he will blast them to smithereens
I should tell you
the puritan in me always carries a shotgun
he wants to punish the world I suppose
because he feels he needs punishing
for who knows how many unpunishable things
like the times as a boy he'd sneak shirtless between the cows
to haul his tongue across the saltlick
or how he'd study his dozing granny's instep
like it was the map of his county
or the spring nights he'd sneak to the garden behind the sleeping house
and strip naked
while upon him lathered the small song
of the ants rasping their tongues
across the peonies' sap, making of his body

a flower-dappled tree
while above him the heavens wheeled and his tongue
drowsed slack as a creek,
on the banks of which, there he is,
right now, the puritan in me
tossing his shotgun into the cattails,
taking off his boots, and washing his feet
in that water.

feet

Friends, mine are ugly feet:
the body's common wreckage
stuffed into boots. The second toe
on the left foot's crooked
enough that when a child
asks *what's that?* of it,
I can without flinch or fear of doubt lie
that a cow stepped on it
which maybe makes them fear cows
for which I repent
in love as I am with those philosophical beasts
who would never smash my feet
nor sneer at them
the way my mother does:
"We always bought you good shoes, honey,"
she says, "You can't blame us
for those things," and for this
and other reasons
I have never indulged in the pleasure
of flip-flops shy or ashamed
digging my toes like ten tiny ostriches into the sand
at the beach with friends
who I'm not sure love me,
though I don't think Tina loved me—
she liked me, I think—but said

to me, as we sat on lawn chairs
beside a pool where I lifeguarded and was meticulous
at obscuring from view with a book or towel
my screwy friends,
You have pretty feet,
in that gaudy, cement-mixer, Levittown accent
that sends all the lemurs scaling my ribcage to see
and she actually *had* pretty feet
and so I took this as a kindness incomparable and probably
fell a little bit in love with her for that afternoon
with the weird white streak in her hair
and her machinegun chatter and her gum snapping
and so slid my feet from beneath my *Powerman and Iron Fist* comic book
into the sun for which they acted like plants opening their tiny mouths
to the food hurtling to them through the solar system,
and like plants you could watch them almost smile,
almost say *thank you*, you could watch them
turn colors, and be, almost, emboldened,
none of which Tina saw
because she was probably digging in her purse
or talking about that hottie on *The Real World*
or yelling at some friend's little sister to put her ass in her trunks
or pouring the crumbs of her Fritos into her thrown open mouth
but do you really think I'm talking to you about my feet?
Of course she's dead: Tina was her name, of leukemia: so I heard—

why else would I try sadly to make music of her unremarkable kindness?
I am trying, I think, to forgive myself
for something I don't know what.
But what I do know is that I love the moment when the poet says
I am trying to do this
or *I am trying to do that.*
Sometimes it's a horseshit trick. But sometimes
it's a way by which the poet says
I wish I could tell you,
truly, of the little factory
in my head: the smokestacks
chuffing, the dandelions
and purslane and willows of sweet clover
prying through the blacktop.
I wish I could tell you
how inside is the steady mumble and clank of machines.
But mostly I wish I could tell you of the footsteps I hear,
more than I can ever count,
all of whose gaits I can discern by listening, closely.
Which promptly disappear
after being lodged again,
here, where we started, in the factory
where loss makes all things
beautiful grow.

smear the queer

was what we called it
sometimes or sometimes
kill the man
from afar
you could watch
the savannah's dust bellow
from the chase
the fleet boy's pronghorn flight
his juke and whirl
his stutter-step spring
or the buffalo boy's chug
hauling the whole
flailing pride
and one way or another
down we'd be
dragged and good chance was
there'd be some piling on
the bloody-knuckled boy
and the long-haired boy
the boy with the crooked
smile and the one
who would die bad
tumbling and swan-diving
in layers and tangles
in fleshy knots of sediment

until was made a mountain
within which a cave
where was heard
a stream's faint murmur
and seen the mirrored glance
of an iridescent bird's
luminous eyes
a cave
across the ridged walls
of which gallops and flickers
a herd of elk
and on the sandy
floor beneath the feathers of firelight
all of us sprawled lank
and shimmering and woven
opening our small
bodies like moonflowers
to the dark

to my best friend's big sister

One never knows
does one
how one comes to be
standing
most ways to naked
in front of one's pal's
big sister who has, simply
by telling me to,
gotten me to shed
all but the scantest
flap of fabric
and twirl before her
like a rotisserie
chicken as she
observes
and offers thoughtful critique
of my just
pubescent physique
which is not
a thing
to behold
what with my damp trunks
clinging to
my damp crotch
and proportion and grace

are words the definition
of which I don't yet know
nor did I ask the
the mini-skirted scientist
sitting open-legged
and now shoeless
on my mom's couch
though it may have been
this morning
while chucking papers
I heard through the Rob Base and DJ EZ Rock
pulsing my walkman
a mourning
dove struggling
snared in the downspout's
mouth and without
lowering the volume
or missing a verse
I crinkled the rusted aluminum
trap enough that with
a little wriggle
it was free
and did not
at once
wobble to some

powerline but sat on my hand
and looked at me
for at least
one verse of "It Takes Two"
sort of bobbing
its head
and cooing once or twice
before flopping off
but that seems very long ago
now
as I pirouette
my hairless and shivering
warble of acne and pudge
burning a hole
in the rug as big sis tosses off
Greek and Latin words
like pectorals and
gluteus maximus
standing to show me
what she means
with her hands on my love
handles and now
I can see myself
trying to add some gaudy flourish
to this memory

to make of it
a fantasy
which is why I linger
hoping to mis-recall
the child
me
make of me
someone I wasn't
make of this
experience the beginning
of a new life
gilded doors
kicked open blaring
trombones a full
beard Isaac Hayes singing in the background
and me thundering forth
on the wild steed
of emergent manhood
but I think this child was not
that child
obscuring, as he was, his breasts
by tucking his hands
into his armpits
and having never even made love
to himself

yet was not
really a candidate for much
besides the chill
of a minor shame
that he would forget for 15 years
one of what would prove
to be many
such shames
stitched together like a quilt
with all its just legible
patterning which could be a thing
heavy and warm
to be buried in
or instead might be held up
to the light
where we see the threads
barely holding
so human and frail
so beautiful and sad and small
from this remove.

armpit

First it's the balm
of light sifting
through the rafters
of the old church
from the neighborhood
I'd break into not for ruckus
but to sit and write
my name in the dust on the pews
and watch the pigeons
roost beside the dozing
and crooked eye of the stained-
glass window the racket
somehow of the street
softened but that
maybe is another poem because
I'm trying to get
to the awkward flock
of flamingoes soaring
somewhere below my navel or
in the back of my throat
or the small house
behind my eyes suddenly
lit up
when sitting in the library's
silent reading room

above her small stack on seed
saving and plant dyes and
kangaroos
a bookish woman's hairy armpit flashes
it is summer it is
hot and those flamingoes
as a small boy before the bus came
I'd leap into the bed
beside my father
and push my face into his armpit
his bird's nest
he called it half-smiling
with a book
in one hand smelling of the night shift
at Pizza Hut
while my mother stood in the doorway
on her way to work
mentioning something about dinner
or maybe the car
though truth is I didn't listen
I just watched
the light glimmer in drifts
between the rafters
making glow somehow the
wide pine boards

and the dove up there
invisible but making
those noises.

spoon

for Don Belton

Who sits like this on the kitchen floor
at two in the morning turning over and over

the small silent body in his hands
with his eyes closed fingering the ornate

tendrils of ivy cast delicately into the spoon
that came home with me eight months ago

from a potluck next door during which
the birthday boy so lush on smoke

and drink and cake made like a baby
and slept on the floor with his thumb

in his mouth until he stumbled through my garden
to my house the next morning where I was frying up

stove top sweet potato biscuits, and making
himself at home as was his way,

after sampling one of my bricks
told me I could add some baking powder

to his and could I put on some coffee
and turn up the Nina Simone and rub, maybe,

his feet, which I did, the baking powder,
stirring it in, and I like to think,

unlikely though it is, those were the finest
biscuits Don ever ate, for there was organic coconut oil

and syrup bought from a hollering man
at the market who wears a rainbow cap

and dances to disguise his sorrow,
and it might be a ridiculous wish,

but the sweet potatoes came from a colony
just beyond my back door, smothering

with their vines the grass and doing their part
to make my yard look ragged and wild

to untrained eyes, the kale and chard so rampant
some stalks unbeknownst drooped into the straw mulch

and the cherry tomatoes shone like ornaments
on a drunken Christmas tree and the blackberry vines

gnawed through their rusty half-ass trellis,
this in Indiana where I am *really* not from, where,

for years, Negroes weren't even allowed entry,
and where the rest stop graffiti might confirm

the endurance of such sentiments, and when
I worried about this to Don on a cool September evening,

worried it might look . . .
Don in his kindness abundant and floral, knowing my anxiety

before I stated it, having been around,
having gone antiquing in Martinsville a few weeks back

and been addressed most unkindly by a passing truck
or two, trucks likely adorned with the stars and bars,

knowing the typhoons race makes our minds do,
twirling with one hand a dreadlock and patting my back with the other

asked, smiling sadly and knowingly, *niggerish?*
before saying, *it looks beautiful*, and returning to some rumination

on the garden boy of his dreams,
whose shorts were very short, and stomach taut

and oily enough to see his reflection in.
Don told me this as we walked arm in arm

through our small neighborhood,
which he asked me if he could do,

is this ok, he asked, knowing mostly
how dense and sharp the dumb fear

of mostly straight boys can be—oh Don—
walking arm in arm, shoulder to shoulder,

his hand almost patting my forearm, resting there,
down the small alley next to the graveyard,

fall beginning to shudder into the leaves,
and Don once dreamt he was in that graveyard

next to his house on 4th, where in real life
we sang Diana Ross's "Missing You" while decorating

his kitchen, where I once asked to borrow
a signed Jamaica Kincaid novel at which

Don made one sound by sucking his teeth that indicated
I was both impossibly stupid and a little bit cute

and in the dream in the graveyard
where century-old oak trees look like giants trudging

into a stiff wind, and some gravestones are old
enough to be illegible and lean back as though

consulting the sun, Don was floating
into the air which, pleasant at first,

became terrifying, he told me, beginning to cry,
just a little, as the world beneath him

grew smaller and smaller, his house
becoming a toy, the trees' huge limbs like the arms,

now, of small people, calling him down,
but he couldn't stop going higher, he said, crying,

just a little, and I have inserted myself
two or three times into the dream, imagining a rope

cinched to his waist by which Don might be tethered
to this world, snatching it as it whips uncoiling

through the grass at my feet, and gripping it
with all my strength until it almost hauls me up

and takes the skin of my palms with it, twisting slowly into the sky
at which I become like the trees here on earth shouting

Come back, come back
running some blocks looking into the sky,

first down 4th, but as the wind sends him this way and that
I too veer through backyards, hopping a fence or two,

not wanting to take my eyes from him,
not wanting to lose him, as he sails

in and out of the low clouds, looking down
with his sad eyes, just as he did

when he said at breakfast *I'm a survivor, I survived*,
this 53-year-old gay black man,

to which we did a little dance
listing the myriad bullets he'd dodged,

swirling the biscuits in their oily syrup,
Don occasionally poking his fork into the air for emphasis,

laughing and sipping coffee and
shaking our heads like we couldn't believe it,

and having survived Don wanted a child to love,
and we made plans that I might make the baby

with my sweetie and he could be the real dad, reading
and cooking and worrying, while I played in the garden

and my sweetheart made the dough,
which maybe would have worked,

though Don never once cleaned a dish, and when I told him
to put his goddamned plate in the sink, he writhed

in his seat and called me bitch before plopping it in,
returning to his Destiny's Child tune about survival,

while he scooped and slurped the remaining batter
with this spoon in my hands, into which I stare, seeing none of this.

I swore when I got into this poem I would convert
this sorrow into some kind of honey with the little musics

I can sometimes make with these scribbled artifacts
of our desolation. I can't even make a metaphor

of my reflection upside down and barely visible
in the spoon. I wish one single thing made sense.

To which I say: *Oh get over yourself.*
That's not the point.

After Don was murdered I dreamt of him,
hugging him and saying *you have to go now,*

fixing his scarf and pulling his wool overcoat snug,
weeping and tugging down his furry Russian cap

to protect his ears, kissing his eyes and cheeks
again and again, *you have to go,*

cinching his coat tight by the lapels,
for which Don peered at me again with those sad eyes,

or through me, or *into* me,
the way my dead do sometimes,

looking straight into their homes,
which hopefully have flowers

in a vase on a big wooden table,
and a comfortable chair or two,

and huge windows through which light
pours to wash clean and make a touch less awful

what forever otherwise will hurt.

weeping

I'm thinking here of the proto-Indo-European root
which means the precise sound of a flower bud

unwrapping, and the tiny racket a seed makes
cracking open in the dark, which has evolved

in a handful of Latinate languages to mean the sound
of lovers exiting each other, implying as well the space

between them which usage is seen first in Dante
in the fourteenth century, elbowing it for good into our mouths

and minds, and of course the sweet bead of sugar
imperceptibly moseying from the fig's tiny eye precisely

unlike sorrow which the assembly of insects sipping there
will tell you, when I tell you my niece, without fit or wail,

knowing her friend Emma had left and not said goodbye,
having spent the better part of the day resting on her finger,

sometimes opening her wings, which were lustrous brown
with gold spots, to steady herself at the child-made

gale, or when she was tossed into the air while my niece
took her turn at pick-up sticks until calling Emma

by holding her finger in the air to which Emma would wobble down,
and Mikayla said *Deal us in* when we broke out the dominoes

at which they made a formidable duo, whispering to each other
instructions, and while the adults babbled our various dooms

Mikayla and Emma went into the bedroom where they sang
and danced and I think I heard Mikayla reading Emma

her favorite book, both of them slapping their thighs, leaning
into each other, and at bedtime Mikayla put on her PJs

carefully, first the left arm through while Emma teetered
on the right, then the other, and in the dark Mikayla whispered to Emma,

who had threaded her many legs into the band of Mikayla's sleeve,
while she drifted, watching Emma's wings slowly open

and close, and Emma must have flown away for good, judging
from the not brutal silence at breakfast, as Mikayla chewed

the waffle goofily with her one front tooth gone, and weakly smiled,
looking into the corners of the room for her friend, for Emma,

who had left without saying goodbye, the tears easily
rolling from her eyes, when I say she was weeping,

when I say she wept.

to the mistake

It is good
to know
a thing or two
about that
of which you
speak or
even to be expert
which is not
requisite though
a thing or two
is good
like the prop plane
I know
is going to land
on the canvas roof
of my friend's
rickety jeep
while the salutatorian
to be sits
in the backseat giddy
with her new
graphing calculator
and the driver
says something
I think

about Arsenio Hall
and he sounds like
a bunny
in an echo chamber
but it's hard
to hear with those
propellers roaring
above and today
I am lecturing
on the miracle
of the mistake
in a poem
that hiccup or weird
gift that spirals
or jettisons
what's dull and land-locked
into as-yet-untraversed i.e. cosmic
(I overuse this metaphor
with my students)
grounds I tell
this to 105 give or take
undergrads who mostly
don't care
and wrestle second
to second the

by now blood-borne
drive to check
their beckoning phones
which mostly
bless them they
don't the mistake
I say is a gift
don't be afraid
see what it teaches you
about what the poem
can be I know
of what
I speak like
the two tabs
of very potent
evidently
acid I
dropped four hours
before this reunion
and graduation party
of sorts for
we the gifted
and talented
corn chips and Mr. Pibb
and store-bought

cookies the texture of which
sunk me knee-deep
in a desert
I imagine
I looked something like
an opaque cloud
that day when
Mr. and Mrs. Simonoski
our brainy hosts
and teachers
guffawed in claymation
the tremendous
bead of spit
balancing on Mr.
Simonoski's lip
before a gust of air
lifted it and it
drifted to the course
fabric of his beard
all the spiny
hairs of which seemed
to screech
like crickets and
no wonder I
declined the invitation

from the volleyball
court although
I was a phys ed major
and beneath the
white arcs the ball
painted in the sky
my classmates, Lisa
and Eugene and Ik
and Becky, all
looked a bit
alien with craniums
engorged slightly
and spines
compressed if not even
serpentine their limbs
flailing about
wildly like cuttlefish
speaking only in
polysyllabics which
must have made my breathy
grunts all the
more apish who
knows where the poem
will lead you
I tell them to let go

their reins
and listen to the tongue's
half-wit
brilliance the corner
of the mind
made light by some
accidental yoking
of two impossibly
joined things
one or two in the rear
I notice their eyes
roll into the backs
of their heads
and my plastic cup
of root beer by now is spilling
a bit while Mr. Simonoski
laughs like a hyena
plunging its face
in a ruptured gut
and nothing has ever been
as clear to me as
the bell that rang in my head that day
we were
a 12-year experiment
the garden-variety
brainiacs from a suburban

school passable genetic
mixture forgettable
location Mr. Sim's oddly large
eyes and his long reptilian tail
now making sense
and the way someone with
an electric can-opener voice
seemed always to be inside him
speaking when he spoke
now making sense
as the night winds down
and the last of the cake
is served writhing with some
fluorescent scrawl
only I seem able to read
while all the good-natured kids
whose fingernails are chewed
raw and jaws pulse
who are so good so
very good
and soon will be hauled into
that bottomless sky
under which I stumble
to see what direction they're coming from
and can I run

ode to sleeping in my clothes

And though I don't mention it
to my mother
or the doctors
with their white coats
it is, in fact,
a great source of happiness,
for me, as I don't
even remove my socks,
and will sometimes
even pull up my hood
and slide my hands deep
in my pockets
and probably moreso
than usual look as if something
bad has happened
my heart blasting a last somersault
or some artery parting
like curtains in a theater
while the cavalry of blood
comes charging through
except unlike
so many of the dead
I must be smiling
there in my denim
and cotton sarcophagus

slightly rank from the day
it is said that Shostakovich slept
with a packed suitcase beneath
his bed and it is said
that black people were snatched
from dark streets and made experiments
of and you and I
both have family whose life
savings are tucked 12 feet beneath
the Norway maple whose roots
splay like the bones
in the foot of a man
who has walked to Youngstown, Ohio
from Arkansas without sleeping
or keeping his name
and it's a miracle
maybe I almost never think of
to rise like this
and simply by sliding my feet into my boots
while the water for coffee
gathers its song
be in the garden
or on the stoop
running, almost,
from nothing.

becoming a horse

It was dragging my hands along its belly,
loosing the bit and wiping the spit
from its mouth made me
a snatch of grass in the thing's maw,
a fly tasting its ear. It was
touching my nose to his made me know
the clover's bloom, my wet eye to his
made me know the long field's secrets.
But it was putting my heart to the horse's that made me know
the sorrow of horses. The sorrow
of a brook creasing a field. The maggot
turning in its corpse. Made me
forsake my thumbs for the sheen of unshod hooves.
And in this way drop my torches.
And in this way drop my knives.
Feel the small song in my chest
swell and my coat glisten and twitch.
And my face grow long.
And these words cast off, at last,
for the slow honest tongue of horses.

sharing with the ants

a euphemism for some
yank and gobble
no doubt some
yummy tumble or other
like monkey-spanking
or hiding the salami
of course your mind
goes there
loosey-goose that you are
me too!   me too!
you have a favorite
don't lie
I've heard you say them
tending the hive
eating the melon
how's the tunnel traffic
or as a "massage therapist"
would say to my pal
when his loneliness
dragged him to a carpeted room
in an apartment building
in Chinatown
where the small hands
lathered his body
open the door

naturally
sharing with the ants
some entymologic metaphor
the chronic yoke
in love making
not only of body to body
but life to death
sharing with the ants
or the specific act of dragging with the tongue
one's sweat-gilded body from the tibia's
lookout along the rope bridge
of the Achilles' marching
across the long plains of the calf
and the meticulously unnamed zone behind the knee
over the hamstring into
use your imagination for Chrissakes
but I will tell you it is dark there
and sweet
sharing with the ants
but that's not at all
what I'm talking about
I mean actually
sharing with the ants
which I did September 21
a Friday in 2012

when by fluke or whim or
prayer I jostled the crotch-high
fig tree whose few fruit had been
scooped by our fat friends
the squirrels
but found shriveled and purple
into an almost testicular papoose
smuggled beneath the fronds
of a few leaves
one stalwart fruit which
I immediately bit in half
only to find a small platoon of ants
twisting in the meat
and when I spit out my bite
another 4 or 5 lay sacked out
their spindly legs
pedaling slow nothing
one barely looking at me through a half-open eye
the way an infant might
curled into its mother's breast
and one stumbled dazed through my beard
tickling me as it tumbled
head over feet over head
over feet back into the bite
in my hand the hooked sabers

of their mandibles made soft kneading
the flesh their claws
heavy and slow with fruit
their armor slathered plush
as the seeds shone above
the sounds of their work
like water slapping
a pier at night
and not one to disrupt an orgy
I mostly gobbled around their nuzzle and slurp
careful not to chomp a reveler
and nibbling one last thread of flesh
noticed a dozy ant nibbling the same
toward me its antennae
just caressing my face
its pincers
slowing at my lips both
of our mouths sugared
and shining both of us
twirling beneath the fig's
seeds spinning like a newly
discovered galaxy
that's been there forever

ending the estrangement

from my mother's sadness, which was,
to me, unbearable, until,
it felt to me
not like what I thought it felt like
to her, and so felt inside myself—like death,
like dying, which I would almost
have rather done, though adding to her sadness
would rather die than do—
but, by sitting still, like what, in fact, it was—
a form of gratitude
which when last it came
drifted like a meadow lit by torches
of cardinal flower, one of whose crimson blooms,
when a hummingbird hovered nearby,
I slipped into my mouth
thereby coaxing the bird
to scrawl on my tongue
its heart's frenzy, its fleet
nectar-questing song,
with whom, with you, dear mother,
I now sing along.

the opening

You might rightly wonder what I am doing here
in the passenger's seat of this teal Mitsubishi

with the hood secured by six or seven thick strips of duct tape,
sitting next to Myself, who sits in the driver's seat,

having quickly pulled into the lot of the Kentucky Fried Chicken
on Rt. 413 in Levittown, Pennsylvania,

from which years ago my father would sometimes
bring home a bucket of hot wings to share

just with me, his comrade in spice and grease and gore,
rattling the little charnel house like a bell

to indicate a joy impending and plucking
the lid to waft the scent toward the vents

into my room where I'd catch a whiff and toss my Avengers
comic to vault down the steps before high-fiving

my smiling old man, stinking of his own hours working
at the Roy Rogers down on Cottman, and plunge into the scuzzy muck,

the two of us silently cleaning the bones while the laugh track
of some rerun ebbed and flowed;

you wonder rightly what it is I am saying
quietly in the ear of Myself, and what I am pointing at

with one hand while the other rests on Myself's shoulder,
tenderly if not a bit tentatively, for Myself

is still a very big man, and quick, and trying hard
not to take anyone with him over the ledge on which he stands,

which you can tell when he just barely looks in my direction
a bit animal with sweat glistening the back of his neck

and his temples, his jaw flexed with his hands
clutching the wheel, the slightest whistle in his breath

while beneath the looming sign of the Colonel smiling
like one concealing some awful and bloody secret

a family in the rearview parks their minivan
and not mostly noticing us makes their way out:

an older brother gripping the wrist of a smaller one
who clutches his purple and yellow jacket; an infant snugged

in its father's arm tipping its head back to see us
from beneath its light blue cap, opening and closing its hand

as the glass doors swing shut behind them.

• • •

You likewise might wonder how Myself has arrived
at this flamboyant terror, an accretion

the way in caves, where nothing without light
is seen, minerals will gather into impossible spires

waiting to impale a thing, that, while driving home
from his dear mother's apartment, he actually saw

in his mind with a clarity like the semis behind him
trudging toward the on-ramp to Philadelphia or New Jersey,

like the carts wandering about the PathMark lot or the woman
in a housedress and slippers waiting at the crosswalk

smoking a cigarette, his own hands working a vial
of some sort from which he poured a poison

into his mother's half-eaten tub of blueberry yogurt,
which imagined matricide is perhaps especially jarring

to Myself, given the awkward walking he does
avoiding ants and other tiny beasts,

given the long prayer he found himself giving
the chickadee that met its death against his windshield,

lodging under the wiper blades and drumming the glass
with the one free wing until he could pull over, whereupon

Myself did kiss the unlucky thing, folding its wings into its body,
before laying it in a small hole at the foot of a dogwood tree

in full regalia, its thousand flowers like a congregation
walking arm in arm in the river.

● ● ●

And knowing Myself well now I can see
what murderous birds flew numerous and hungry

into the attic, shrikes especially, working
their ways in at the slimmest shims of light

between shingles and through rotholes wedging first
their heads in without blinking and collapsing

the bones of their bodies their tongues thrust out
and necks made long wriggling in leaving behind

clumps of shivering feathers blood-glued to the cracks
one after the next prying through loose boards

snapping at the tail feathers of the ones in front of them
the clawing feet skitting in one after the next

until the attic roared with soaring and the war
screams of birds clutching one another with talons

by the neck or back and veering quick
toward any piercing barb or thorn

or snapped branch jeering into the air like this
the impaled thing writhing and fluttering

once or twice its wings and twisting open its beak
from which came no sound—

which is, in fact, the wrong metaphor, the more I think of it,
for the birds in question favor the long view

of open meadows. They love exposed perches on which they fasten
their talons and unwrap their beautiful wings in the wind.

And the birds I'm talking about are not birds at all,
but common sorrow made murderous simply by nailing

the shingles tight, and caulking with the tar always boiling out back
all possible cracks. Which is to say, the metaphor here

has become the sealing up as much as any bird, has become
the way Myself had made unwittingly a habit of slathering

mortar everywhere, almost by accident,
for fear of what might forever slip in and be felt;

which was, in addition to everything else, simply, goddamn,
how sad my mother was when my father died, goddamn,

how sad was Myself; and how scared was Myself,
scared nearly, in fact, to death, at his mother afraid

or not sleeping well or not unpacking for months in her new apartment,
outside of which Myself, visiting, would sit in his car

for a half hour or more, staring
into the yellow aluminum siding's patina and the seam

it made with the fake white brick
as he felt the bones of his chest breaking which was the feeling

of the very real terror he had at what his hands might do, which his hands
would never do, which was like the wood shake helpless against the prying

shrike, clawing and snapping its hunter's beak, which, I am happy
to remind us both again, was not the feeling at all. All Myself was feeling,

in fact, was not feeling his heart break again and again.
The way he did for some time sitting with his mother

in her living room, watching the Eagles that year have a good season
while she sobbed and didn't sleep well and in some way

shone in her sorrow complete though it was very hard
for him to admire for the roaring in his head, which was nothing

more, it turns out, than the sounds of not weeping, the sounds
of sadness turned back. Nothing savage, nothing cruel or vicious,

not a bird in sight—just sadness. Which is to say,
in other words, just being alive.

• • •

My Beloved Chickenshit; My Sweet
Little Chickenshit; don't run,
My Baby. Don't flee, My Honey.
Hunker down. Hunker down.

• • •

There is, in my yard, a huge and beautiful peach tree.
I planted the thing as a three-foot whip,

a spindly prayer with a tangle of roots so delicate,
so wild, I took ten minutes to feather them apart

before spreading them in the hole like a lightning storm
in one of those images of the brain. Now the tree reaches almost

into the grumpy neighbor out back's yard, the one who once
snarled at me and my house *why would anyone paint a house that color?*,

and whose unsmiling middle-aged daughter mows the lawn
twice a day, though I've seen in March or April

when the tree's myriad pink mouths unfurl
and blow kisses to everyone in sight, the burdened curl

of the old lady's back uncoil—I've seen her stand up some and wink
at that tree, and, no kidding, saw her once teeter out

in a gloomy gray pantsuit and, scrubbed by the bloom,
change her costume right then and there to something

frilled and blazing, which she wore on her trot
through the neighborhood whistling to the birds swirling

behind her. In this neck of the woods you have to prune
a peach tree if you don't want the fruit to rot, if you don't want

all that fragrant grandstanding to be for naught. Which is why
today, this sunny April afternoon with no rain or real freeze forecasted,

I dig out my tools and sharpening stone, making the blades
all shimmer enough to skim the hair from my arm.

Then, after cleaning each with a rag dipped in
some watered-down bleach, I move around the tree's

sprawling limbs, the ruddy young growth all wagging
at the sun, all shivering with the breezes

muscling through. And with my loppers and snips
I look up into the behemoth tree and begin clipping,

first the wisps of growth and pencil thick
sprouts, rubbing off with my thumb tiny leaf buds

peeking from the trunk, before hauling myself into the tree,
wedging my boot in the sturdy crotch and clinging

to a fat branch to keep thinning: overlapping
limbs or those with some hint of disease; those grown haywire

or deranged twisting toward the light; and those from which
last year grew maybe half a bushel of fruit, limbs

wrist thick with bark whorled and cleft by age,
but whose tight angle might snap this year

and wreck the tree, and require a saw to remove, which I do,
watching the last branch tumble into the pile of clippings below.

I do this again and again, crawling through the branches
as though through a beloved's ribs. Friends, if you haven't guessed,

every time I do this a little bit I mourn,
leaning the pruner's steel flush against the flesh,

or working back and forth the saw's grin and feeling
the smooth wood tumble or twirl into the little tomb which, after

the cutting is done, is about my size—is about the size,
give or take, of everyone I've ever loved. This is how, every spring,

I promise the fruit will swell with sugar: by bringing in the air and light—
until, like the old-timers say, the tree is open enough

for a bird to fly through. Which, in fact, they do—two cardinals
flirting; a blue jay flashing its pompadour; one of those little grayish
birds

I can't remember the name of, landing on the furthest limbs
where it does nothing special besides maybe dump its teeny

chamber pot while whistling this very ditty:
half dirge, half disco, some giggly trill

loop-de-looping from its tiny beak,
while its ruffled, musty body sways on the tree's furthest finger,

resting exactly where I put it,
singing just as I asked it to,

which, from up here, where the newly open view is good, I can see
is what I was pointing to, what I was saying quietly to Myself,

in the parking lot of the KFC in Levittown, Pennsylvania,
as Myself shivered, and looked up, trying to see,

trying to hear.

c'mon!

My mother is not the wings,
nor the bird, but the moon
across the laced hands
of the nest. The palm on a fever-dreamer's
brow. She was born a crab, waving
the twin flags of her pinchers.
That's one of those poetry lies. Truth is
my poor mom's hands bruised on our butts,
so that was the end of that.
And when the monk slapped her ass,
she didn't kick him down the stairs,
but slipped the saffron tale
in her pocket. Truth is my mother's brave
as a bison. For years
she dragged her hooves through the ash
of her heart. Head down. Steam rising
in ghosts from her pelt. Years
where nary a blade of grass. Nary
birdsong. But one day
a small seed took hold. Then another.
Soon, beetles and spiders came back, and then,
and then, the birds were chatting
in the new growth. And right now
a family of elk crosses a stream
and behind them on a hillside

a galaxy of wildflowers
shimmers. Shimmers
and hollers,
"C'mon!"

to the mulberry tree

Everyone knows it's good luck
if inconvenient
when a bird shits on you
but even moreso
good luck if the bird shits on you
when you're plucking
gold currant tomatoes
sweet enough to make your bare feet
lift just so
off the ground
and the beetles beneath scurry
and giggle
and as I move to gobble one
mouth agape and swooped in a grin at once
the shit slurries half in
and half on my
sun-warmed chin which
forgive me
jiggles me from my reverie
for I am only human
swiping the slurp of turd from my mouth
only to see it is mostly
purple the goop seedy and gelatinous
and when I see the bird pitching
his swill from the branch above

I know that yes this shit
is mostly berry from
that most prolific of trees
which some numbskulls
call a weed because it's so prolific
and not, they say, particularly
useful, these same some
call insipid the mulberry's flavor which
I think means tasteless
or bland but given
I detect swirled in the shit
the sweet of the thing
insipid doesn't fit the bill
but rather most likely describes
the sex life of the describer
but why should I get personal
defending a tree's honor
mostly I'm happy the birds
feast on the top-most branches
of these tall trees and leave be
for the time being
my blueberries and soon blackberries
and grapes and these little tomatoes
though to be sure
it is a certain glee

as spring gasps into summer
and the lowest branches
shimmer with their simple booty
which I must jump for and sometimes
high which I will not, probably,
always be able to do, for jumping
and grabbing at once like this
a soft thing is hard
be gentle
she said emerging from the dugout beneath the mulberry tree
where the big kids gathered
and we mostly rode our bikes by fast
so as not to be snatched to the ground and pummeled
or worse for they were *teenagers*
but I knew this early July morning they would be nowhere
to be found and the tree
would be burdened
with a crop begging to be loosed
on my ice cream
she wiped her eyes and yawned
and put on glasses
and there was in her hair
a small sprig of grass
and she was barefoot
laughing and filling with me slowly my bucket

eating a few when it was full
giggling at the small burst of juice one made
on her chin
and behind her beneath the tree
there was a filthy blanket
and a pack of cigarettes
and tinfoil wrappers crumpled and shimmering
and the frayed remnants of a rope
and seeing me seeing
into the terrible future
she put softly one hand on my chin
and the other in my hair
turning my head away from what wreckage
waited in there
and back into the leaves,
which too I will do to you,
so that none of us will ever die terribly,
but stay always like this, lips and fingers blushed purple,
the faint sugar ghosting our mouths,
beneath the tree inside me,
which is the same tree now grown inside you:
the three of us snugged in the canopy
on our tippy-toes, gathering fruit
for good.

ode to drinking water from my hands

which today, in the garden,
I'd forgotten
I'd known and more
forgotten
I'd learned and was taught this
by my grandfather
who, in the midst of arranging
and watering
the small bouquets
on mostly the freshest graves
saw my thirst
and cranked the rusty red pump
bringing forth
from what sounded like the gravelly throat
of an animal
a frigid torrent
and with his hands made a lagoon
from which he drank
and then I drank
before he cranked again
making of my hands, now,
a fountain in which I can see
the silty bottom
drifting while I drink
and drink and

my grandfather waters the flowers
on the graves
among which are his
and his wife's
unfinished and patient, glistening
after he rinses the bird shit
from his wife's
and the pump exhales
and I drink
to the bottom of my fountain
and join him
in his work.

wedding poem

for Keith and Jen

Friends I am here to modestly report
seeing in an orchard
in my town
a goldfinch kissing
a sunflower
again and again
dangling upside down
by its tiny claws
steadying itself by snapping open
like an old-timey fan
its wings
again and again,
until, swooning, it tumbled off
and swooped back to the very same perch,
where the sunflower curled its giant
swirling of seeds
around the bird and leaned back
to admire the soft wind
nudging the bird's plumage,
and friends I could see
the points on the flower's stately crown
soften and curl inward
as it almost indiscernibly lifted
the food of its body
to the bird's nuzzling mouth

whose fervor
I could hear from
oh 20 or 30 feet away
and see from the tiny hulls
that sailed from their
good racket,
which good racket, I have to say,
was making me blush,
and rock up on my tippy-toes,
and just barely purse my lips
with what I realize now
was being, simply, glad,
which such love,
if we let it,
makes us feel.

catalog of unabashed gratitude

Friends, will you bear with me today,
for I have awakened
from a dream in which a robin
made with its shabby wings a kind of veil
behind which it shimmied and stomped something from the south
of Spain, its breast aflare,
looking me dead in the eye
from the branch that grew into my window,
coochie-cooing my chin,
the bird shuffling its little talons left, then right,
while the leaves bristled
against the plaster wall, two of them drifting
onto my blanket while the bird
opened and closed its wings like a matador
giving up on murder,
jutting its beak, turning a circle,
and flashing, again,
the ruddy bombast of its breast
by which I knew upon waking
it was telling me
in no uncertain terms
to bellow forth the tubas and sousaphones,
the whole rusty brass band of gratitude
not quite dormant in my belly—
it said so in a human voice,

"Bellow forth"—
and who among us could ignore such odd
and precise counsel?

Hear ye! hear ye! I am here
to holler that I have hauled tons—by which I don't mean lots,
I mean *tons*—of cow shit
and stood ankle deep in swales of maggots
swirling the spent beer grains
the brewery man was good enough to dump off
holding his nose, for they smell very bad,
but make the compost writhe giddy and lick its lips,
twirling dung with my pitchfork
again and again
with hundreds and hundreds of other people,
we dreamt an orchard this way,
furrowing our brows,
and hauling our wheelbarrows,
and sweating through our shirts,
and less than a year later there was a party
at which trees were sunk into the well-fed earth,
one of which, a liberty apple, after being watered in
was tamped by a baby barefoot
with a bow hanging in her hair
biting her lip in her joyous work

and friends this is the realest place I know,
it makes me squirm like a worm I am so grateful,
you could ride your bike there
or roller skate or catch the bus
there is a fence and a gate twisted by hand,
there is a fig tree taller than you in Indiana,
it will make you gasp.
It might make you want to stay alive even, thank you;

and thank you
for not taking my pal when the engine
of his mind dragged him
to swig fistfuls of Xanax and a bottle or two of booze,
and thank you for taking my father
a few years after his own father went down thank you
mercy, mercy, thank you
for not smoking meth with your mother
oh thank you thank you
for leaving and for coming back,
and thank you for what inside my friends'
love bursts like a throng of roadside goldenrod
gleaming into the world,
likely hauling a shovel with her
like one named Aralee ought,
with hands big as a horse's,

and who, like one named Aralee ought,
will laugh time to time til the juice
runs from her nose; oh
thank you
for the way a small thing's wail makes
the milk or what once was milk
in us gather into horses
huckle-buckling across a field;

and thank you, friends, when last spring
the hyacinth bells rang
and the crocuses flaunted
their upturned skirts, and a quiet roved
the beehive which when I entered
were snugged two or three dead
fist-sized clutches of bees between the frames,
almost clinging to one another,
this one's tiny head pushed
into another's tiny wing,
one's forelegs resting on another's face,
the translucent paper of their wings fluttering
beneath my breath and when
a few dropped to the frames beneath:
honey; and after falling down to cry,
everything's glacial shine.

And thank *you*, too. And thanks
for the corduroy couch I have put you on.
Put your feet up. Here's a light blanket,
a pillow, dear one,
for I think this is going to be long.
I can't stop
my gratitude, which includes, dear reader,
you, for staying here with me,
for moving your lips just so as I speak.
Here is a cup of tea. I have spooned honey into it.

And thank you the tiny bee's shadow
perusing these words as I write them.
And the way my love talks quietly
when in the hive,
so quietly, in fact, you cannot hear her
but only notice barely her lips moving
in conversation. Thank you what does not scare her
in me, but makes her reach my way. Thank you the love
she is which hurts sometimes. And the time
she misremembered elephants
in one of my poems which, oh, here
they come, garlanded with morning glory and wisteria
blooms, trombones all the way down to the river.
Thank you the quiet

in which the river bends around the elephant's
solemn trunk, polishing stones, floating
on its gentle back
the flock of geese flying overhead.

And to the quick and gentle flocking
of men to the old lady falling down
on the corner of Fairmount and 18th, holding patiently
with the softest parts of their hands
her cane and purple hat,
gathering for her the contents of her purse
and touching her shoulder and elbow;
thank you the cockeyed court
on which in a half-court 3 vs. 3 we oldheads
made of some runny-nosed kids
a shambles, and the 61-year-old
after flipping a reverse layup off a back door cut
from my no-look pass to seal the game
ripped off his shirt and threw punches at the gods
and hollered at the kids to admire the pacemaker's scar
grinning across his chest; thank you
the glad accordion's wheeze
in the chest; thank you the bagpipes.

Thank you to the woman barefoot in a gaudy dress
for stopping her car in the middle of the road
and the tractor trailer behind her, and the van behind it,
whisking a turtle off the road.
Thank you god of gaudy.
Thank you paisley panties.
Thank you the organ up my dress.
Thank you the sheer dress you wore kneeling in my dream
at the creek's edge and the light
swimming through it. The koi kissing
halos into the glassy air.
The room in my mind with the blinds drawn
where we nearly injure each other
crawling into the shawl of the other's body.
Thank you for saying it plain:
fuck each other dumb.

And you, again, you, for the true kindness
it has been for you to remain awake
with me like this, nodding time to time
and making that noise which I take to mean
yes, or, *I understand*, or, *please go on*
but not too long, or, *why are you spitting*
so much, or, *easy Tiger*
hands to yourself. I am excitable.

I am sorry. I am grateful.
I just want us to be friends now, forever.
Take this bowl of blackberries from the garden.
The sun has made them warm.
I picked them just for you. I promise
I will try to stay on my side of the couch.

And thank you the baggie of dreadlocks I found in a drawer
while washing and folding the clothes of our murdered friend;
the photo in which his arm slung
around the sign to "the trail of silences"; thank you
the way before he died he held
his hands open to us; for coming back
in a waft of incense or in the shape of a boy
in another city looking
from between his mother's legs,
or disappearing into the stacks after brushing by;
for moseying back in dreams where,
seeing us lost and scared
he put his hand on our shoulders
and pointed us to the temple across town;

and thank you to the man all night long
hosing a mist on his early-bloomed
peach tree so that the hard frost

not waste the crop, the ice
in his beard and the ghosts
lifting from him when the warming sun
told him *sleep now*; thank you
the ancestor who loved you
before she knew you
by smuggling seeds into her braid for the long
journey, who loved you
before he knew you by putting
a walnut tree in the ground, who loved you
before she knew you by not slaughtering
the land; thank you
who did not bulldoze the ancient grove
of dates and olives,
who sailed his keys into the ocean
and walked softly home; who did not fire, who did not
plunge the head into the toilet, who said *stop,*
don't do that; who lifted some broken
someone up; who volunteered
the way a plant birthed of the reseeding plant
is called a *volunteer*, like the plum tree
that marched beside the raised bed
in my garden, like the arugula that marched
itself between the blueberries,
nary a bayonet, nary an army, nary a nation,

which usage of the word volunteer
familiar to gardeners the wide world
made my pal shout "Oh!" and dance
and plunge his knuckles
into the lush soil before gobbling two strawberries
and digging a song from his guitar
made of wood from a tree someone planted, thank you;

thank you zinnia, and gooseberry, rudbeckia
and pawpaw, Ashmead's kernel, cockscomb
and scarlet runner, feverfew and lemonbalm;
thank you knitbone and sweetgrass and sunchoke
and false indigo whose petals stammered apart
by bumblebees good lord please give me a minute...
and moonglow and catkin and crookneck
and painted tongue and seedpod and johnny jump-up;
thank you what in us rackets glad
what gladrackets us;

and thank you, too, this knuckleheaded heart, this pelican heart,
this gap-toothed heart flinging open its gaudy maw
to the sky, oh clumsy, oh bumblefucked,
oh giddy, oh dumbstruck,
oh rickshaw, oh goat twisting
its head at me from my peach tree's highest branch,

balanced impossibly gobbling the last fruit,
its tongue working like an engine,
a lone sweet drop tumbling by some miracle
into my mouth like the smell of someone I've loved;
heart like an elephant screaming
at the bones of its dead;
heart like the lady on the bus
dressed head to toe in gold, the sun
shivering her shiny boots, singing
Erykah Badu to herself
leaning her head against the window;

and thank you the way my father one time came back in a dream
by plucking the two cables beneath my chin
like a bass fiddle's strings
and played me until I woke singing,
no kidding, singing, smiling,
thank you, thank you,
stumbling into the garden where
the Juneberry's flowers had burst open
like the bells of French horns, the lily
my mother and I planted oozed into the air,
the bazillion ants labored in their earthen workshops
below, the collard greens waved in the wind

like the sails of ships, and the wasps
swam in the mint bloom's viscous swill;

and you, again you, for hanging tight, dear friend.
I know I can be long-winded sometimes.
I want so badly to rub the sponge of gratitude
over every last thing, including you, which, yes, awkward,
the suds in your ear and armpit, the little sparkling gems
slipping into your eye. Soon it will be over,

which is precisely what the child in my dream said,
holding my hand, pointing at the roiling sea and the sky
hurtling our way like so many buffalo,
who said *it's much worse than we think,*
and sooner; to whom I said
no duh child in my dreams, what do you think
this singing and shuddering is,
what this screaming and reaching and dancing
and crying is, other than loving
what every second goes away?
Goodbye, I mean to say.
And thank you. Every day.

last will and testament

You thought somehow you were off the hook,
which was naïve if not dumb
though I will not berate you
given as this poem is in fact me on my knees
to beg of you a small grody chore
and though you may not know the ways
my lucky body corrodes
nor what stray bricks heaved
from what stray roofs
are headed my way—nor I yours—
degrade I do and so
am here to plead the lucky sod—
lover, pal, niece, mom—Lord God,
please not mom—charged with heaving
my luggage to chuck the gore
straight into the orchard.
Beats me by dry flame
or cauldron deep, by your granny's
mortar and pestle to grind
my bones and teeth having flayed
and woven of my flesh two or three
mats of mulch; do the good work
with your pickaxe
or hacksaw, oh for god's sake
have a little fun

with this grave and grizzly drill
and know I'm giggling too
and feel nary a thing;
and when you've lopped what needs lopping,
(Oh use the hand pruners
with the red handle; they were my favorite!
Such elegant recoil! Such scintillant snips!)
chuck my at last acheless feet to the fickle peach;
my hands upturned and open
to the village of figs where the ants pray
for fruit slather-faced; my jawbone
yoked to its tongue planted as a small forgiveness
of stupid, lonely, frightened Samson—and his
stupid, lonely, frightened God—and as some meager balm
to the donkey he defamed—give that
to the black mulberry,
tree of forgiveness, tree
of bounty; lob my head and its vaults
of perfectly useless mudge
to the persimmon, where the bleak cold
coaxes forth the sugars
shining in the long dark, and my heart
go ahead and tuck beneath
some comfrey sprawling across the plum tree's feet,
so I might dance a long and loamy tango

with my old man. Lord knows I don't wish to go
just yet, for the flush of flowers
and then fruit blooms me into a cartwheel
that whirls for weeks,
not to mention my knees' little ditties are still mostly pretty,
and good lord the funks
I stumble over lust-drunk and hungry
walking the streets of most cities
and some days wake up tonguing
the laminated pages of the world map—
but when I do head out
I won't be like the old man
who wept as he died,
wheeled through his orchard the last time,
whispering *goodbye, goodbye,*
running his thin hands
over the gnarled twining of vines,
listening this last time to the wind
through his lemons and oranges,
the occasional thump of wind-fallen fruit,
the night's scarce light unspooling through the leaves,
goodbye child, goodbye little one, he says,
teetering out of his chair to clutch
and rub his neck and cheek
against the calloused bulk of the olive,

which curls into him, the one
lank branch cradling him,
its thin leaves whispering—
for some days I can't wait
to sling my gangly bulk into the peach blossom's sheer camisoles,
or to become the frilly skirts
of the pear which wind-blown heave
the syrupy smell of semen
and oh the joy I will be
wafting into the noses and tongues of passersby
who will furrow their brows
before, some of them, crafting their various rackets
with their loves or themselves
thanks in no small part to me
or to shimmy into the pawpaw's steeple
where my rank bloom
tongue kissed by flies
puckers at the gorgeous world
its brazenly human lips,
not to mention, yes, of course,
to be gobbled by folks the likes of whom
I've never imagined, I'm saying
I'm saying to gift of my body some pure glee
which, living, I don't know
that I ever did . . . except last spring

distracting the neighbor cat just enough
to free the hummingbird in its paws,
or the ramshackle salsa my pal and I stepped
at a café in Greece where the music was good
and the white-aproned workers stomped
and howled and sent us off
with bags of cookies,
oh, and maybe another thing or two,
but you get my point, friend,
which, getting to, I know, was a long row to hoe,
though I'm simply extolling
your transubstantiative gift to me
and whomever's heart will be a little broke
when I kick it,
but if you think this was blabber-mouthed,
you better buckle in
when I kick it.

acknowledgments

Some of the poems in this book were previously published in the following magazines. I am grateful to the editors.

"Burial" and "Patience" in *Solstice*; "Wedding Poem" and "Sharing with the Ants" in *Timber*; "Feet" in *Gabby*; "To My Best Friend's Big Sister" on the Academy of American Poets' *Poem-A-Day*; "Ode to the Fig Tree on 9th and Christian" and "To the Puritan in Me" in *American Poetry Review*; "Ode to the Mistake" in *Forklift, Ohio*; "Becoming a Horse" in the *Sun*; "Ode to Drinking Water from My Hands" in *Exit 7*; "Ode to Sleeping in My Clothes" in *Massachusetts Review*; "Ode to the Flute" in *Nashville Review*; "Ode to Buttoning My Shirt" in *Bombay Gin*; "Spoon" in *Lit*; "Opening" in *Oversound*; "Weeping" in *Gulf Coast*; "C'mon!" and "Last Will and Testament" in *Kinfolks: A Journal of Black Expression*; "Catalog of Unabashed Gratitude" in *Waxwing*; "Ending the Estrangement" in *Taos Journal of International Poetry and Art*.

"To the Fig Tree on 9th and Christian" was included in *The Best American Poetry 2014*. I am grateful to David Lehman and Terrance Hayes for that.

I am grateful to a number of people whose fingerprints are all over these poems. Among them are Curtis Bauer, Remica Bingham, Alex Chambers, Nandi Comer, Ruth Ellen Kocher, Victor Lau, Jennifer Leonard, Keith Leonard, Bryce Martin, Chris Mattingly, Aimee Nezhukumatathil, Michael Simmons, Dave Torneo, David Waters, and Simone White.

I am grateful, too, to Stephanie Smith, whose eyes and ears and heart on and in these poems has been indispensable. Who, in fact, knew some of these poems might be of use before I did. Thank you.

And to Aracelis Girmay and Patrick Rosal, boats and anchors in the deep water: always, thank you.

And to the people who have listened to these poems at readings, and have thereby helped me to make them with the little sounds you did or didn't make: thank you.

Thank you to Tia Ari for sharing with us the beautiful painting on the cover.

To Cave Canem. To the Bread Loaf Writer's Conference. To the Vermont Studio Center. Thank you.

Thank you to Ed Ochester for believing in this book.

Thank you to the Bloomington Community Orchard which is the ground from which so many of these poems grow. To the family that place has grown to be. Love, and thank you.

And to YOU, reader: thanks!